MIDNIGHT MUSINGS

NATASHA SAEDNEJAD

*To all the daydreamers, night owls, and travellers
on their journey home to themselves.*

CONTENTS

INTRODUCTION

If you've found this book then I'd like to think it wasn't
by accident.

Perhaps you'll read these pages and paragraphs and feel
like you've finally been seen.

Perhaps these poems will inspire you to put your feelings
into prose.

Perhaps these short stories will nudge you tell your own
that you've kept hidden inside.

Whatever it is that you get from this book, just know
that these midnight musings have come straight from my
soul to yours.

Dip into them whenever you feel the call to, sit and let
them speak to your Soul, and just know that I am
sending warmth to you through my words.

Nati

HOW?

How do I begin to tell the story of this life of mine?
32 years in the making,
Yet it still feels so…
Unmade.

How does one put into words this feeling of being so
rudderless,
So unmoored,
And yet so rooted to the spot?

When did everyone else grow up,
Build lives,
Loves,
Legacies,
Whilst I was still searching for shore?

When did the voice in my head,
The one that speaks in doubts and derogatives,
Become the one steering the ship?

Which words will suffice to fill this hole of longing,

Wanting,

Yearning,

For time to stand still,

Yet rush forward towards my future?

In every decision I see a potential me,

In every memory a lost little girl,

How do I find the me of the present moment,

With a compass fixed on the future

Or pointing to the past?

How do I continue to tell the story of this life of mine?

Do I lament time lost,

Or rejoice at the years that reach forward?

Do I cower to the criticisms in my head,

Or do I rise with rebuttals and reclamations of my

power?

How do I begin to tell the story of this life of mine,

When it's still being written?

WHO

Who are you when no one's watching?
Who are you at 3am when the world is still and silent?
What do you see when you stop and look in the mirror?
Can you look yourself deep in the eyes?

What do you feel when you touch your skin and map
out the contours of your body?
Can you be that close and gentle with yourself?

Who were you before society got a grip on you?
What did you dream of doing before you were put in the
maze of modern life?

Where did you want to go before life tied you down?
Where are you now? Are you happy here?

Can you hear your Soul or is it drowned out by the
voices around you?

Can you sit with yourself and come face to face with the
You that lives inside?
Can you bring that You to the surface and celebrate
them?

Can you get to know, love and learn all there is to know
about them?
Can you let the You within you fly?

There are wings ready to unfurl and soar in your Soul.
It's time, angel.

DEAR YOUNGER ME

I'm so sorry they hurt you,
Took your voice away,
Took you choice away,
It was never theirs to take.

My heart breaks for every time you felt you weren't good
enough,
Clever enough,
Beautiful enough,
Enough.

I cry for every tear your shed over someone who didn't
even see them,
See you,
Value you.

I scream for every time you were silenced,
Made to feel less than,
Shrunk to fit into someone else's box.

My body hurts from every battle you fought,
From the weight you had to carry,
That wasn't yours.

I can't change the past,
I can't erase your pain,
But I can give you a safe space now,
To let it all out.

I can hold you through the night,
While we howl together,
Heal together,
Breathe together,
Be together.

I can take you with me,
While we live out all yours dreams,
And face all your fears.

I can't promise there'll be no more pain,
I can't promise we'll find all the answers,
But I can promise you
That you'll never feel alone again,
And you'll always know
Just how much I love you.

YOU

And I will come back to you,
No matter how far you stray into the dark,
No matter how long you stay standing under clouds,
And no matter how many battles you feel you must face
alone.

I will come back.

I know you feel lost,
I know you feel low,
I know you feel that you're wrapped in weeds while
others blossom and grow,
But just know this, my love…

The caterpillar does not know the beautiful butterfly it
will become,
It only sees the darkness.
It does not know that it will emerge into a world of
beauty and bliss,
It just feels solitude and seclusion.

This incarnation was never meant to be easy,
The path never meant to be flat,
For it's only after climbing the mountains that you can
bring powerful perspective to this earthly plane.

But, my beautiful warrior,
Neither were you meant to fight so hard,
Without reprieve.
Don't you think, perhaps, it's time to lower you shield,
And put down your sword?

No battles are won when the army is pushed to breaking,
No breakthroughs come from pushing past the need to
stop,
To listen,
To silence the opinions of others,
And turn up the volume of your Soul.

Only then will you hear your calling,
Only then will you know the truth...

That you were never meant for the ordinary,
And the only person you ever need to make proud
Is you.

HOLD ON

Hold on, my love,
Through the struggle comes the serenity,
Through the pain comes the peace.

An eclipse may block the light,
But in brings forth what lay in the shadows.
The power in our darkness,
The hidden talents we've yet to cherish.

An earthquake breaks ground to reveal what lies beneath,
Waves come to ride us to new shores,
And this darkness will amplify our light.

So hold on, my love,
You're so close to the light on the other side.

WILL

I won't worship you above myself.

I don't believe in putting your needs before my own.

I won't love you more than I love myself.

I don't need you to complete me or to be my 'other half'.

I will honour all that is good and great in you.

I will support you as you grow, while I grow too.

I will love you with the ferocity that I learned to love myself.

I will be a whole soul who loves you soulfully.

We will respect the entry into each other's energy,

We will stand together in fertile soil as we grow towards the stars.

We will share the love we show to ourselves,

We will come together as two to create forever.

BREATHE

Breathe,
It's the breath that will bring you back.
When all else is spinning,
And your mind's lost in a maze,
Breathe to find the space to stop,
And come back to your centre.

Close your eyes,
Drop your shoulders,
And breathe bright energy right down into your belly.
Feel The Universe enter through your crown,
Pour down through your chakras,
And flow out of the soles of your feet,
Grounding you in its peaceful energy.

Release the breath from the belly up,
Exhaling all that's stagnant,
All that's heavy,
All that's trapped,
And see it rise up and out of your being,
And away from your aura.

Feel your heartbeat slow
As you sink into surrender,
And remember that the only thing you need to do right
now,
Is breathe.

FULL MOON

With every Full Moon,
We're reminded of the beauty that comes from growth,
The light that emerges from darkness,
The strength that lay behind the shadows.

It lies behind ours too.

With every Full Moon,
We look up with wonder,
As if for the first time,
And stop to gaze for a while.

Shouldn't we look at ourselves in the same way too?

With every Full Moon,
We try our best to harness her energy,
To honour her presence,
However fleetingly full it may be.

Can't we honour our ebbs and flows in the same way?
There is much to be learnt from this big, beautiful ball,
But perhaps the biggest and most beautiful lesson of
them all is that...

On days when you feel like a waning crescent,
Or even totally eclipsed,
Your emptiness is just a trick of the light-
For you are always whole,
Always powerful,
Always capable of turning tides...

Sometimes we all just have to rest in the shade for a
while to power up our full shine.

I

And I will hold you
Through the good and the bad,
Through the calm and the storm,
In the valley and up the mountains,
In the silence and through the screams.

When you feel alone,
Close your eyes and listen
To me beat within you,
To my breath stir your chest,
To hum of my Soul rise from the deep.

If the days get darker,
And the nights never-ending,
Let me trace the tracks of your tears,
Lace your fingers into mine,
And lead you to your light.

No one knows you better,
No one ever will,
From ball of light to human life,
I've lived inside,
Never doubting you for a second.

If you'd only let me love you more,
Let me show you more compassion,
You'd never feel alone again,
Never wonder if you're loved -

Because I am you
And you are me
And together, we are everything we'll ever need

POWER

When your light takes up space,
And small minds try to make you smaller,
Stand tall in your purpose.

When they try to silence your voice,
Because its truth and authenticity deafens their ego,
Shout louder from your Soul.

When your light shines into the eyes of those who live
with theirs half-closed,
They'll attempt to close the blinds on you.
Shine brighter.

Pure power and purpose intimidates those those who use
it diluted with darkness,
But yours is more potent,
More powerful,
More pervasive,
Because you live in the light.

As they try to push us into a corner,

Censor our words,

Stifle our creativity,

Push back with the power that resides in your love,

In your light,

In your life's purpose - to be a burning beacon of the power that comes from peace, perspective, and protecting your energy when it's under attack.

Because they can try to silence us, but there is no match for the volume that comes from speaking straight from your Soul and Source.

BURN

Remember to keep burning furiously bright, my love,
Shine light in the eyes of those who wish to keep you in
the dark.
Let your flames rise up and carry you with them,
Swept up to Source on swirls of smoke.
This fire within you was made to rage and roar,
Burning away debris and dust,
The fertile ashes soil to your Soulful dreams.
Fear not the heat of your fire,
For it's the furnace from which you'll rise like a phoenix,
Ready to take flight,
Fanning the flames that will propel you towards your
purpose.
Keep burning furiously bright, my love,
A fire full of fantasy, force, and fortune.

EMBRACE

Embrace your body,
Every divine dimple,
Every cosmic curve,
Every starlit scar.
You are The Universe,
Expressing itself in human form,
Every inch of your skin
Is soulful stardust,
Designed to be celebrated,
Welcomed on Earth to be worshipped.
So be bountiful with your love for your body,
Sense your Soul sing through your sensuality,
And never let anyone cover your curves in shame.
You have been magically made,
And your body is yours and yours alone
To show and shine

SHE

Do not approach her
Without preparing to worship.
Do not touch her
Without reverence in your fingertips.

Her body is a temple
Her Soul is your altar
Her aura a cloud of heaven-sent sanctity.

It is in bowing to her
That she will submit to you.
In respecting her worth
That she will honour you.

She is holiness
Sin
The unspeakable
The enshrined
In one body and Soul.

She is the giver of life
Protector of energy
And a force of nature.

Thunderbolts bend around her
Rain drips from her mouth
As clouds part with her lips
And oceans flow from between her legs.

She is the beginning and the end
The alpha and the omega
The source of pure pleasure
And the vengeance that makes the earth quake.

She is your dream and darkest thought in exquisite
harmony
Writhing around your mind with supple sensuality
Waiting for you to step into her waters
And drown in her divinity.

PLEASURE

Do you see my skin as an opportunity to sexualise me?
My sexuality as an open invitation for unwanted
attention?
Does the attention you give it make me attention-
seeking?

When I show my body, does that make it yours to
interact with?
Objectify?
Cover with crude comments?
And when I don't respond in kind,
Does that make me a tease?

How do I explain to you
That my sexuality is mine
And mine alone?
That by expressing it
I'm interacting sexually with myself,
Not laying bare an open invitation?

If it's done on a public platform,
Does that make my body property of the public?
Or is it my profile to show what's mine?
To celebrate myself,
Show myself my beauty,
And to show you -

That I will never see my body and my beauty through
your eyes,
Never reduce myself to simply an object of your pleasure,
But always find pleasure in knowing that I am a body,
A brain,
A Soul,
Here to bring endless pleasure to myself.

MUSE

Pursue me,
Pave a path with intentions and effort.

Woo me,
With words and worthy actions.

Spoil me,
Shower me with seduction and softness.

Desire me,
Deeply for both my dark and my light.

Worship me,
For my wisdom, my womb, my witchcraft.

No longer will I feel guilt
For wanting to be worshipped.

No longer will I feel weak
For wanting protection and power from a partner.
No longer will I find feminism
At odds with wanting to be looked after.

For all my partner gives
I give back tenfold.
From my heart,
From my Soul,
From my body.

This holy trinity is a blessing,
And I am the vixen vessel
Who carries it to you.

Such potent power deserves praise,
Protection,
Powerful admiration,
And perennial celebration.

I will no long settle for crumbs,
When I deserve the cake,
The confetti,
The constant compassion,
The consistent communication,
And the enduring devotion of an artist to his muse.

SOMEONE

Someone who can start a fire, but can calm those flames with soft tides of emotion and affection.

Someone who makes my heart race but who can also slow the racing thoughts in my head.

Someone whose roots anchor us while we grow, but don't weigh us down when we want to fly.

Someone whose presence is strong and steadfast, but soft and supple when needs be.

Someone who has access to my body, but wants to seduce my mind and Soul first.

Someone who wants to contemplate the stars, but also sees magic in the mundane.

Someone who can explore every part of me, but never fear when the landscape changes.

Someone who can leave me breathless, but breathe life into the parts of me I thought I'd lost.

Someone secure when solitary, but even more powerful when in a pair.

Someone who hasn't found their way to me yet, but who will be entirely worth the wait.

ENERGY

Sexual energy is freedom and fire.

Healing and happiness.

Sensuality and spirituality.

Body and beyond body.

It is coming home to ourselves, and allowing others in.

It is meeting ourselves out in the depths and inviting others to swim in our deep.

It is connecting body with Soul and human with Higher.

It is creation, connection, exploration and explosiveness.

It is all four elements combined.

The passion of Fire.

The emotional flow and fluidity of Water.

The corporeal connection of Earth.

The blissful breeze of inspiration of Air.

It is the creator, the created, and the creative.

It is power, in its purest form.

THE DREAM

Safety.

Strength.

Space to flow.

Room to grow.

Pillars for my emotion-filled ivy to wrap around.

Strong arms that wrap around me.

Compassion.

Passion.

Depth and deliverance of both word and deed.

An open mind and an open heart that fiercely guards
mine.

Touch.

Time.

The time to be patient with a guarded heart and walled-
off wounds.

Leadership that lets my femininity lead when called to.

Protection.

Power.

Peace.

ABOUT THE AUTHOR

Nati is a writer, tarot reader, and intuitive healer from Surrey, United Kingdom. Having started her professional life as a French and Spanish tutor, she began to feel the call to help others in a more spiritual and holistic way, whilst also embracing her love of writing.

This brought her to begin her spiritual work as a tarot reader and healer, and start sharing her poetry and writing. Nati is also an advocate of embracing your sexuality, and shares this message through her posts on Instagram.

Midnight Musings is her first poetry anthology, which she hopes will be one of many, and she is thrilled to share it with you.

You can follow her and find on more on Instagram:

@nati_saednejad

Printed in Great Britain
by Amazon